CW00590120

Meet ...
the animals from

MADAGASCAR

ESCAPE 2 AFRICA

Alex, Marty, Gloria and Melman are very good friends. They live in New York Zoo. They ran away from New York and came to Madagascar.

I'm Melman the giraffe.

I'm Alex the lion.

I'm Marty the zebra.

Melman

Alex

I'm Gloria the hippo.

Marty

Gloria

New Words

fight

The lions are **fighting**.

country

Africa is a beautiful **country**.

mark

The cat has a black **mark**.

dam

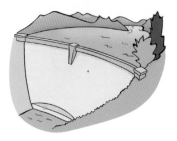

There is a lot of water in the **dam**.

pilot

A **pilot** flies a plane.

4

plane

The **plane** is flying.

water hole

The hippos are in the **water hole**.

reserve

Here is a bus on a **reserve** in Africa.

'Welcome!'

Welcome to my house!

show

This is a dance **show**.

Verbs

Present	Past
fly	flew
take	took
stand up	stood up

A long time ago ...

Alex lived in a hot country. Alex was a young lion and his dad was King. Alex liked dancing but his dad was not happy.

'Don't dance, Alex! Fight!' his dad said.

Alex had a mark on his hand. His dad had a mark too.

'You are my boy,' said Alex's dad. 'Everyone can see that.'

One day, some men came. Alex's dad didn't see them. The men took Alex away. Alex's new home was in New York. He never saw his mum and dad again.

Alex was happy in New York. He had some good friends there – Marty, Gloria and Melman.

One day, they all went to Madagascar …

CHAPTER ONE
'We're going home!'

Alex, Marty, Gloria and Melman had a great time in Madagascar. Now it was time to go home.

'Come and see us in New York!' Alex shouted to their friends.

'We're going home!' laughed Marty.

But their plane was very old and it flew very slowly ...

'We're coming down!' said the pilot.

'Great!' said Alex. 'That was quick!'

'No!' shouted the pilot. 'We're coming down NOW!'

'Help!' shouted Alex. 'This is horrible!'

The plane came down.

CRASH!

'Is everyone OK?' asked Marty.
They were in a very hot place.
'We're OK, but the plane isn't!' said Gloria.
'But we're all here and we're all friends,' said
Marty.

Some people stopped and took pictures of the animals. Alex took an old woman's bag and ran. Her phone was in the bag.

'Yes!' laughed Alex. 'Now we can find help and go home!'

But the phone didn't work.

'Come and look at this, everyone!' said Marty.

They were in a very beautiful country. But where were they?

'I know this place,' said Alex.

'Africa!' said Marty. 'It's Africa!'

CHAPTER TWO
The show

The four friends walked and walked. Suddenly they saw a lot of animals in front of them.

'Hello!' said Alex. 'I'm Alex.'

An old lion came close.

'I am King Zuba,' said an old lion. 'We don't want more animals here. Go home!'

'Wait!' said the lion next to him. 'Alakay?' she said. 'Is it you?'

Alex didn't understand. 'No,' he said. 'I'm Alex.'

King Zuba opened Alex's hand. There was the mark.

'My boy!' he said. 'He's home!'

Alex looked at King Zuba's mark.

'Mum and Dad!' he laughed.

'Zuba!' shouted a lion.

It was Makunga. Zuba didn't like this lion.

'Is your boy going to be in the pride?' he asked. 'Is he strong and quick? Let's see tomorrow – in front of all the lions!'

Zuba was not happy.

'It's OK, Dad!' said Alex. 'In New York I do a lot of shows. It's not a problem.'

Next morning, all the lions came to see Alex.

'Who is going to be in the show with Alex?' said
King Zuba.

A very big lion stood up. 'Let's start!' he shouted.

'Great!' said Alex. He started dancing. He was
very good.

'No!' shouted the lion. 'Let's start … fighting!'

Alex opened his eyes.

'Are you OK?' his mum asked him.

'No, I'm not OK,' said Alex. 'I don't fight. I dance.'

'He can't be in the pride!' said Makunga.

Alex's dad was very sad. 'Then I am also not in the pride. I can't be King.'

Alex, his mum and his dad walked slowly away.

'Now I am King!' laughed Makunga.

Moto Moto was a very strong hippo. He liked Gloria.

'Come to the water hole with me!' he said.

'OK!' said Gloria.

But Melman saw them.

'Listen, Moto Moto,' he said. 'Be very nice to Gloria. She's a beautiful woman and a great friend.'

Next day, there was a problem. There was not much water in the water hole.

'Who is going to have the water?' asked the animals.

'We can fight for it!' said Makunga.

'No!' said Alex. 'I'm going out of the reserve. I'm going to find water for everyone.'

'Wait, Alex!' shouted Marty. 'I'm coming too!'

CHAPTER THREE
'Welcome to the pride!'

Alex and Marty walked and walked.

'Look!' shouted Alex. 'There's no water because of that!'

Marty looked. It was a dam.

Suddenly an old woman was behind Alex.

'Bad lion!' she shouted. 'You took my bag!'

'Oh no!' Alex started running. 'Find help, Marty!'

'Do you love Moto Moto?' Melman asked Gloria.

'No, Melman,' said Gloria. She looked into his eyes. 'You are the man for me!'

Suddenly Marty was in front of them.

'Come quick!' he said. 'It's Alex!'

'Now I've got you!' said the old woman. 'And I want you for my dinner!'

Alex was frightened.

Suddenly an angry lion ran at the old woman. It was Zuba!

'Let's go, Alex!' he shouted.

'We can't!' said Alex.

There were people all around them.

Suddenly Alex started dancing. 'Come on, Dad!' he said. 'Dance!'

'Look! The lions are dancing!' shouted everyone. The old woman laughed too.

'Alex! Quick! Jump in!'

Alex looked up. It was Marty, Melman and Gloria. They were in the old plane!

Alex and Zuba jumped into the plane. They flew away.

'Break the dam!' Alex shouted to the pilot.

When Alex and Zuba came back to the reserve, there was water in the water hole again. All the animals were very happy.

'Alex and our King are home again,' they shouted. 'Welcome to the pride!'

THE END

AFRICAN LIONS

A long time ago there were lions in all of Africa. Today there are not so many lions.

Africa

■ = lions live here

Did you know ...?

🪶 You can hear a lion's roar 8 kilometres away.

🪶 Lions sleep for 16 to 20 hours a day.

🪶 Lions can live four or five days with no water.

The pride

A pride has ten to twelve female lions, their young lions and two or three male lions.

female

male

The hunt

Lions hunt zebras, giraffes and hippos. So in *Madagascar*, Alex's friends are unusual! The female lions usually hunt. Young lions start hunting when they are about one year old.

★ Do you know any more big cats? ★

Reserves

Many lions in Africa now live in reserves. Some people hunt lions, but you can't hunt animals in a reserve. People can come and look at the lions in the reserves.

What do these words mean? Find out.

roar hunt unusual usually

PHOTOCOPIABLE

After you read

1 Match the names with the sentences.

a) The old woman   i) likes dancing.

b) Makunga   ii) is a very strong hippo.

c) Alex   iii) finds the dam with Alex.

d) Melman   iv) wants Alex for her dinner.

e) Marty   v) loves Gloria.

f) Moto Moto   vi) does not like Zuba.

2 True (✓) or False (✗)? Write in the box.

a) The plane was new.   ☒

b) Alex was happy in the plane.   ☐

c) The plane came down in New York.   ☐

d) Zuba had a mark on his hand.   ☐

e) Gloria went to the water hole with Moto Moto.   ☐

f) Alex liked fighting.   ☐

g) At the end of the story, Makunga was King.   ☐

Where's the popcorn?
Look in your book.
Can you find it?

Puzzle time!

PHOTOCOPIABLE

1 Find seven words in the water hole. The words are from pages 4 and 5.

2 Draw pictures of the animals. Use the letters of the words in the pictures.

giraffe

zebra

hippo

lion

3 Which words describe the characters?

beautiful   big

happy   black and white

long legs   nice

strong   tall

beautiful
....
....
....

beautiful
....
....
....

beautiful
....
....
....

4a Which is your favourite animal? Tick your favourite and then ask your friends.

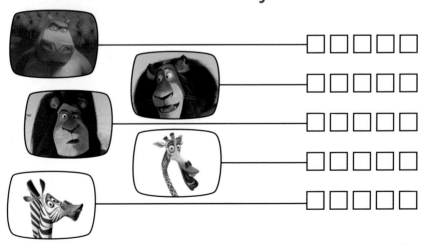

b Which animal has more ticks? ....

Imagine ...

In pairs, mime a scene from the book. Your friends guess who you are, what you are doing and what you are saying.

Example:

> Who are we?

> You are Alex and his dad.

> What are we doing?

> You are dancing.

> What are we saying?

> Zuba says, 'Don't dance! Fight!'

Chant

1 🎵 **Listen and read.**

Welcome to the pride!

Africa is beautiful.
Welcome to the pride!
Beautiful and hot.
Welcome to the pride!

Alex is a lion.
Welcome to the pride!
A lion and a dancer.
Welcome to the pride!

Zuba is the King.
Welcome to the pride!
A king and a dad.
Welcome to the pride!

Alex does not fight.
Welcome to the pride!
Does not fight his friends.
Welcome to the pride!

Alex finds the water.
Welcome to the pride!
The water for the animals.
Welcome to the pride!

2 🎵 **Say the chant.**